People in My Community/La gente de mi comunidad

Crossing Guard/ El guardia de cruce

JoAnn Early Macken
photographs by/fotografías de Gregg Andersen

Reading consultant/Consultora de lectura: Susan Nations, M.Ed., author/literacy coach/consultant

WEEKLY WR READER®
EARLY LEARNING LIBRARY

Please visit our web site at: www.earlyliteracy.cc
For a free color catalog describing Weekly Reader® Early Learning Library's
list of high-quality books, call 1-877-445-5824 (USA) or 1-800-387-3178 (Canada).
Weekly Reader® Early Learning Library's fax: (414) 336-0164.

Library of Congress Cataloging-in-Publication Data available upon request
from publisher. Fax (414) 336-0157 for the attention of the Publishing
Records Department.

ISBN 0-8368-3671-5 (lib. bdg.)
ISBN 0-8368-3685-5 (softcover)

First published in 2003 by
Weekly Reader® Early Learning Library
330 West Olive Street, Suite 100
Milwaukee, WI 53212 USA

Copyright © 2003 by Weekly Reader® Early Learning Library

Art direction: Tammy Gruenewald
Page layout: Katherine A. Goedheer
Photographer: Gregg Andersen
Editorial assistant: Diane Laska-Swanke
Translators: Colleen Coffey and Consuelo Carrillo

Printed in the United States of America

1 2 3 4 5 6 7 8 9 07 06 05 04 03

Note to Educators and Parents

Reading is such an exciting adventure for young children! They are beginning to integrate their oral language skills with written language. To encourage children along the path to early literacy, books must be colorful, engaging, and interesting; they should invite the young reader to explore both the print and the pictures.

People in My Community is a new series designed to help children read about the world around them. In each book young readers will learn interesting facts about some familiar community helpers.

Each book is specially designed to support the young reader in the reading process. The familiar topics are appealing to young children and invite them to read — and re-read — again and again. The full-color photographs and enhanced text further support the student during the reading process.

In addition to serving as wonderful picture books in schools, libraries, homes, and other places where children learn to love reading, these books are specifically intended to be read within an instructional guided reading group. This small group setting allows beginning readers to work with a fluent adult model as they make meaning from the text. After children develop fluency with the text and content, the book can be read independently. Children and adults alike will find these books supportive, engaging, and fun!

Una nota a los educadores y a los padres

¡La lectura es una emocionante aventura para los niños! En esta etapa están comenzando a integrar su manejo del lenguaje oral con el lenguaje escrito. Para fomentar la lectura desde una temprana edad, los libros deben ser vistosos, atractivos e interesantes; deben invitar al joven lector a explorar tanto el texto como las ilustraciones.

La gente de mi comunidad es una nueva serie pensada para ayudar a los niños a conocer el mundo que los rodea. En cada libro, los jóvenes lectores conocerán datos interesantes sobre el trabajo de distintas personas de la comunidad.

Cada libro ha sido especialmente diseñado para facilitar el proceso de lectura. La familiaridad con los temas tratados atrae la atención de los niños y los invita a leer — y releer — una y otra vez. Las fotografías a todo color y el tipo de letra facilitan aún más al estudiante el proceso de lectura.

Además de servir como fantásticos libros ilustrados en la escuela, la biblioteca, el hogar y otros lugares donde los niños aprenden a amar la lectura, estos libros han sido concebidos específicamente para ser leídos en grupos de instrucción guiada. Este contexto de grupos pequeños permite que los niños que se inician en la lectura trabajen con un adulto cuya fluidez les sirve de modelo para comprender el texto. Una vez que se han familiarizado con el texto y el contenido, los niños pueden leer los libros por su cuenta. ¡Tanto niños como adultos encontrarán que estos libros son útiles, entretenidos y divertidos!

— Susan Nations, M.Ed., author, literacy coach,
and consultant in literacy development

A crossing guard helps children walk to school safely. He stops traffic so children can cross the street.

— — — — — — —

El guardia de cruce ayuda a los niños a llegar a la escuela de forma segura. El detiene el tráfico para que puedan cruzar la calle.

Children wait on the sidewalk until the crossing guard tells them to walk.

– – – – – – – –

Los niños esperan en la acera hasta que el guardia les indica cuándo deben cruzar.

A crossing guard holds a **flag** or a stop sign. Flags and stop signs tell drivers to stop.

El guardia de cruce lleva una **bandera** o una señal que dice pare. Las banderas y señales que dicen pare, les indican a los conductores que deben detenerse.

flag/bandera

Cars, trucks, and buses stop and wait. Then the school crossing guard tells children it is safe to cross the street.

— — — — — — — —

Los coches, los camiones y los autobuses se detienen y esperan. Después la guardia de cruce dice a los niños que pueden cruzar la calle.

Sometimes, the crossing guard walks with the children to make sure they cross safely.

— — — — — — — —

Algunas veces el guardia de cruce camina con los niños para asegurarse de que crucen la calle de manera segura.

A crossing guard wears a bright **vest**, sash, or raincoat. Drivers can see the bright colors.

- - - - - - - -

El guardia de cruce lleva un **chaleco** brillante, una banda, o un impermeable. Los conductores pueden ver los colores brillantes.

vest/chaleco

15

Crossing guards must learn safety rules. They must know how to signal traffic to stop and go.

- - - - - - - -

Los guardias de cruce deben aprender las normas de seguridad. Tienen que saber dar la señal al tráfico para que se detenga y siga.

Do you know how to cross a street safely? Always cross at a corner. Wait on the **curb**, and look both ways for cars.

━ ━ ━ ━ ━ ━ ━ ━

¿Sabes cruzar la calle en forma segura? Siempre cruza en la esquina. Espera en el **borde de la acera** y mira a los dos lados para ver si vienen coches.

curb/borde
de la acera

19

Never run into a street or an alley. Listen to your school crossing guard. Be safe!

——————

Nunca corras hacia la calle o hacia el callejón. Escucha al guardia de cruce. ¡Ten cuidado!

Glossary/Glosario

sash — a band worn over one shoulder or around the waist

banda — faja o cinta que se lleva sobre un hombro o alrededor de la cintura

signal — make a movement that sends a message

señalar — hacer un movimiento para enviar un mensaje

traffic — cars, trucks, buses, and other things moving on the street

tráfico — coches, camiones, autobuses y otras cosas que se mueven en la calle

vest — a short, sleeveless jacket

chaleco — chaqueta corta sin mangas

For More Information/Más información

Fiction Books/Libros de ficción

Rathman, Peggy. *Officer Buckle and Gloria.*
  New York: G. P. Putnam's Sons, 1995.
Rockwell, Anne F. *Career Day.* New York:
  HarperCollins Publishers, 2000.

Nonfiction Books/Libros de no ficción

DeGezelle, Terri. *School Crossing Guards.*
  Mankato, Minn.: Bridgestone Books, 2002.
Loewen, Nancy. *Traffic Safety.* Chanhassen,
  Minn.: The Child's World, 1996.

Web Sites/Páginas Web

Safety Tips for Walkers

www.nhtsa.dot.gov/kids/biketour/pedsafety/index.html
Department of Transportation page about pedestrian safety

Index/Índice

About the Author/Información sobre la autora

JoAnn Early Macken is the author of children's poetry, two rhyming picture books, *Cats on Judy* and *Sing-Along Song* and various other nonfiction series. She teaches children to write poetry and received the Barbara Juster Esbensen 2000 Poetry Teaching Award. JoAnn is a graduate of the MFA in Writing for Children Program at Vermont College. She lives in Wisconsin with her husband and their two sons.

JoAnn Early Macken es autora de poesía para niños. Ha escrito dos libros de rimas con ilustraciones, *Cats on Judy* y *Sing-Along Song* y otras series de libros educativos para niños. Ella enseña a los niños a escribir poesía y ha ganado el Premio Barbara Juster Esbensen en el año 2000. JoAnn se graduó con el título de "MFA" en el programa de escritura infantil de Vermont College. Vive en Wisconsin con su esposo y sus dos hijos.